BIBLE TEACHING SHEETS THE OLD TESTAMENT
KJV EDITION

ISBN: 978-1-953489-19-7
©2023 Wildrose Media. USA.

All rights reserved. No part of this publication may be reproduced, distributed or transmitted in any form or by any means without prior written permission of the publisher except in the case of brief quotations for critical reviews and certain other noncommercial uses permitted by copyright law.
Title font is *Canted FX* by Nils Cordes.
Font licensed under Creative Commons Attribution-Share Alike 4.0 International License.

Wildrose Media

www.wildrose-media.com

YOU MAY ALSO BE INTERESTED IN:

Simple Sermon Notes for Kids ages 6-8
ISBN: 978-1-953489-09-8
ISBN: 978-1-953489-14-2

AVAILABLE ON AMAZON

Wildrose Media

www.wildrose-media.com

BIBLE TEACHING SHEETS
THE OLD TESTAMENT
KJV EDITION

GENESIS

Literary Style: Historical Narrative, Law

OLD Testament Book # **1** # of chapters **50**

Author: Attributed to Moses.

Audience: Likely written between 1445-1405 B.C.
Contains prophecies of a Messiah who will redeem God's chosen people, the Jews.

Setting: Ancient Mesopotamia, the Fertile Crescent Israel, Palestine, Syria, Lebanon, Iran, Iraq, and Egypt.
The book begins at creation and ends around 1800 B.C.

Of Interest: The word *Genesis* means 'origins', and 'in the beginning'.
First book of the Pentateuch 'five scrolls', also called the Torah.

General Information about the book of GENESIS:
Genesis gives us an understanding of who God is, what His intentions were for the world.
This book can be divided into two parts, Primeval History (creation) and Patriarchal History (covenants).
Genesis begins with God speaking the world into being.
He created Adam (*man or son of earth*) from the dust of the Earth, then appointed him caretaker of the Earth.
He established the seasons, the patterns of night and day, and rest on the seventh day.
He was pleased with His creation, declaring it good.
In chapter 3 God shares his plan for the redemption of mankind, Jesus.
God made covenants (promises) with Adam, Noah, Abraham (Abram), and Jacob (Israel).

Content Highlights:
- The Creation of the world
- Sin enters the world through Adam and Eve's disobedience
- God cleanses the Earth, Noah and the Flood
- The Tower of Babel, and the scattering of nations
- Abraham (Abram) & Sarah (Sarai)
- Isaac & Rebekah
- Jacob (Israel), his wives - Leah & Rachel, and their servants Bilhah & Zilpah
- Joseph

In the beginning God created the heaven and the earth.

Genesis 1:1

Note:
- Lucifer was an angel, he wanted to be like God, as a result of his pride he was kicked out of heaven. He took 1/3 of the angels with him.
- Lucifer means *light-bearer*
- Death began when sin entered the world, making macro evolution an impossibility.

KEY Verses:
- 1:26-31
- 2:7
- 2:18-24
- 3:1-24
- 6:3
- 7:1, 13 - 8:22
- 9:1, 8-17
- 11:1-9
- 12:1-3
- 32:28
- 37
- 41:39-49
- 46:1-25
- 47:27-31
- 50:15-19

Theme: The sovereignty of God.
Redemption and reconciliation is possible through God's grace.

©2023 Wildrose Media

EXODUS

Literary Style: Historical Narrative, Law

OLD Testament Book #: 2 | # of chapters: 40

Author: Moses (see 24:3, Mark 12:26). Moses was 80 years old when he led the Hebrews out of Egypt.

Audience: Likely written between 1445-1405 B.C.

Setting: Ancient Mesopotamia, Egypt, Midian, Red Sea, Mount Sinai. Begins with death of Joseph c. 1880 B.C. & ends with the building of the Tabernacle, around 1445 B.C.

Of Interest: The word *Exodus* means 'exit' or 'departure'. Second book of the Pentateuch, also called the Torah.

General Information about the book of EXODUS:
- Jacob's descendants lived in Egypt for 430 years before the Exodus (see 12:40)
- Several routes have been proposed and scholars disagree where the Red Sea crossing occurred.
- Foreshadowing: the coming Messiah, Jesus Christ. God offers freedom from bondage (sin), dwells in the tabernacle tent among His chosen people (NT- as the Holy Spirit within believers).
- God establishes a covenantal relationship with Israel, identifying them as set apart, a holy nation.

Content Highlights:
- Begins with a brief genealogy of Jacob's family, then describes how the Israelites became slaves in Egypt.
- Introduces Moses; his rescue by Pharaoh's daughter, escape to Midian, calling by God at the Burning Bush
- Moses returns to Egypt- the 10 Plagues, the first Passover, and the Feast of Unleavened Bread
- The Flight from Egypt, crossing the Red Sea, drowning of Pharaoh's army, songs of praise
- Three days' journey to Mount Sinai, grumbling by the Israelites. God provides water, manna & quail
- At Mount Sinai – the 10 Commandments and other laws, the Covenant with Israel, and the Golden Calf
- Instructions for priests, sacrifice, and Sabbath-day worship
- Building of the Tabernacle, the Ark of the Covenant

Note:
- Calculated from the information in 1 Kings 6:1, it is believed that the Exodus occurred in 1446 B.C. Based on these dates, Pharaoh's Thutmose III and his son Amenhotep II were the Hebrew's oppressors.
- Some scholars believe the Exodus occurred later, around 1290 B.C. under Ramses II as his name is mentioned in Exodus 1:11

I am the Lord thy God, which have brought thee out of the land of Egypt, out of the house of bondage. Thou shalt have no other gods before me.

Exodus 20:2-3

KEY Verses:
- 2:23-25
- 3:2-6
- 3:14-17
- 4:29-31
- 6:6-8
- 13:8-9
- 13:21-22
- 14:29-31
- 15:2
- 20:1-17
- 23:20-22
- 28:29-30
- 34:5-7
- 40:34-38

Theme: Rescue, relationship, and redemption.

©2023 Wildrose Media

LEVITICUS

Literary Style: Historical Narrative, Law

OLD Testament Book #: **3**
# of chapters: **27**

Author: Attributed to Moses.

Audience: Likely written between 1445-1405 B.C. Written to the Levite priests and God's chosen people, the Israelites.

Setting: The Israelites are camped at the base of Mount Sinai. Circa 1445 B.C.

Of Interest: The word *Leviticus* means 'about the Levites'. Levi was one of Jacob's 12 sons. Third book of the Pentateuch, also called the Torah.

General Information about the book of LEVITICUS:
- Leviticus is a book of rules which God required His priests, the Levites to follow. Though all of Israel was to be a holy nation set apart from the world, the priests had special requirements and rules to live by.
- Moses' older brother Aaron was appointed Israel's' first high priest. His sons were also ordained.
- The rules addressed in Leviticus include worship, sacrifices, cleanliness, special feast days, and the Sabbath.
- The rules were to help the people worship their holy God, and live holy lives.

Content Highlights:
- Offering types and instructions (burnt, grain, fellowship, sin, guilt)
- The priest's portion of the offerings
- The appointment and consecration of Aaron and his sons as priests
- The disobedience and death of Aaron's sons, Nadab and Abihu
- Laws of Cleanliness
- The Day of Atonement
- Guidelines for holy living
- Laws about holy days, festivals and the Year of Jubilee
- Blessings and punishments
- Rules about vows and gifts

Note:
- The sacrifices in Leviticus foreshadow the ultimate sacrifice of Jesus Christ. We, due to our sinful nature deserved the death penalty. God in His love and mercy sent his sinless son, Jesus to die in our place (substitutionary atonement).
- In contrast to the daily priestly offerings, Christ's death occurred once, and His blood sacrifice is sufficient for all who believe in Him as Savior.

For I am the Lord your God: ye shall therefore sanctify yourselves, and ye shall be holy; for I am holy.

Leviticus 11:44a

KEY Verses:
- 1:2-3
- 10:10-11
- 16:34
- 17:11
- 18:4-5
- 19:2
- 20:26
- 22:3
- 23:22
- 25:10-11
- 26:3-6
- 26:14-17
- 26:38-39
- 27:30

Theme: The holiness of God and God's requirements for His chosen people.

©2023 Wildrose Media

NUMBERS

Literary Style: Historical Narrative, Law

OLD Testament Book #: 4
# of chapters: 36

Author: Attributed to Moses (see 33:2).

Audience: Likely written between 1445-1405 B.C. Written to the Israelites who were about to enter the promised land.

Setting: The book of Numbers begins about 1 year after the Israelites left Egypt. Covers the 39 years wandering in the wilderness, the plains of Moab, and arrival at the Jordan River.

Of Interest: The title comes from the census, or numbering of the people of Israel in this book (ch. 1, 3 & 26). Fourth book of the Pentateuch, also called the Torah.

General Information about the book of NUMBERS:
- Written to teach the next generation of Israelites about God's holiness, and His requirements for them, as they were to inhabit the Promised Land.
- The Israelite children became the inhabitants of the land of Canaan due to their parents' disobedience. When the Israelites refused to enter Canaan, God declared everyone age 20 and older would not enter the promised land, except for Caleb and Joshua (see chapter 14).
- Events in chapters 1-14 took place the first year after the Israelites left Egypt.
- Everything after chapter 20 occurred in the fortieth year after the Israelites left Egypt.
- The stages of their journey are found in chapter 33.

Content Highlights:
- A census of the tribes of Israel. The men numbered over 600,000.
- The arrangement of the tribal camps, redemption of the firstborn sons
- The Kohathites
- Purity laws and regulations for worship, including the vow of the Nazarite
- Israelites leave Sinai headed to the Promised Land, the exploration of Canaan by the twelve spies
- Complaints, disobedience, and rebellion of the Israelites (including Moses & Aaron) towards the Lord
- The blessing of Balaam and the renewed obedience of (second-generation) Israel toward the Lord
- Preparations to conquer Canaan

Note:
- The distance from Egypt to Canaan can be covered in about one week.
- The Kohathites were a branch of the Levites tasked with transporting the tabernacle furnishings
- Moses was permitted to view Canaan from a hill but not to enter as he too had been disobedient to God.

The Lord bless thee, and keep thee: the Lord make his face shine upon thee and be gracious unto thee: The Lord lift up His countenance upon thee, and give thee peace.

Numbers 6:24-26

KEY Verses:
- 1:51-53
- 3:5-8
- 5:1-3
- 7:89
- 12:5-8
- 14:6-9
- 14:18
- 14:26-31
- 17:1-5, 8
- 21:4-9
- 23:19
- 24:17
- 27:12-14
- 27:18-20
- 30:2
- 35:6-8
- 35:34

Theme: There are consequences for disobedience.

©2023 Wildrose Media

DEUTERONOMY

Literary Style: Historical Narrative, Summary, Law

OLD Testament Book #: 5
# of chapters: 34

Author: Written by Moses, except for the chapter about his death, which may have been written by Joshua.

Audience: Written to the Israelites just before they enter the Promised land.

Setting: The Israelites are camped east of the Jordan River preparing to enter Canaan, the Promised Land. Events occur in one location over a few weeks, after 40 years of wandering. (1405 B.C.)

Of Interest: The word *Deuteronomy* means 'second law'. The Law is taught to a new generation. Fifth and final book of the Pentateuch, also called the Torah or Law.

General Information about the book of DEUTERONOMY:

Moses addresses the second-generation Israelites, those who will enter the land of Canaan.

He reminds them of God's covenant and to love, serve, and obey God.

Moses reminds them of the blessings which they can expect if they remain faithful and the curses which will come if they are disobedient.

Moses recites the laws which are to govern the land. These laws are designed to set Israel apart from neighboring nations as a holy nation chosen by God.

Content Highlights:
- The history of Israel, told to the Israelites in a speech by Moses
- Moses reminds the Israelites of the Law, the Sinaitic Covenant
- Cities of Refuge
- Rules for daily living in the Promised Land
- The consequences of covenant-keeping and covenant-breaking
- Joshua becomes leader of the Israelites
- The Song of Moses, and Moses blesses the people of Israel
- The death of Moses

And the Lord, he it is that doth go before thee; he will be with thee, he will not fail thee, neither forsake thee: fear not, neither be dismayed.

Deuteronomy 31:8

Note:
- Though the book's title is 'second law' it is not a new law rather an explanation of the law given to the Israelites in Exodus.
- Moses is 120 years old when he gives these speeches, a few weeks prior to his death.

KEY Verses:
- 1:8
- 3:21-22
- 4:1-2
- 4:20
- 4:39-40
- 5:32-33
- 6:4-5
- 7:6
- 7:9
- 8:19-20
- 10:12
- 18:22
- 28:10
- 30:19
- 31:6

Theme: God's people are called to be holy, set apart from the world.

©2023 Wildrose Media

JOSHUA

Literary Style: Historical Narrative

OLD Testament Book #: **6**   # of chapters: **24**

Author: Much of this book is attributed to Joshua though the author is not named. Joshua had been born into captivity in Egypt and experienced the Exodus. He was about 90 years old.

Audience: Likely written between 1405 - 1385 B.C.

Setting: The plains of Moab to Canaan. Begins with the death of Moses c. 1405 B.C. and ends with the death of Joshua, around 1385 B.C.

Of Interest: The name *Joshua* is synonymous with the name *Jesus*.

General Information about the book of JOSHUA:

Joshua was tasked with dividing the land up among the Israelites, though Reuben, Gad, and the half-tribe of Manasseh had already claimed land east of the Jordan River.

The Levites were given 48 cities, strategically placed in each tribal territory so the people could have access to the priests no matter where they lived.

Content Highlights:
- Preparation to enter the Promised Land
- Rahab and the Spies
- Crossing the Jordan River
- Circumcision of Israelite males born during the wilderness wanderings
- The Fall of Jericho
- Conquering Canaan
- The Sun Stands Still
- Division of the land among the tribes
- Cities of Refuge
- Joshua's farewell
- Covenant renewal at Shechem
- Joshua's death and burial

Note:
- Joshua's given name was Hoshea *salvation*. Moses renamed him Joshua which means *YAHWEH is salvation* (Numbers 13:16).
- Joshua is the first book of prophets in the Tanakh (the Jewish Bible).
- After Joshua dies God appoints judges as leaders to guide Israel.

KEY Verses:
- 1:8
- 1:9
- 6:26-27
- 10:13-14
- 11:23
- 21:43-45
- 23:6-8
- 24:14-15
- 24:32

> Have not I commanded thee? Be strong and of a good courage; be not afraid, neither be thou dismayed: for the LORD thy God is with thee whithersoever thou goest.
>
> Joshua 1:9

Theme: God keeps His promises.

©2023 Wildrose Media

JUDGES

Literary Style: Historical Narrative

OLD Testament Book # **7** | # of chapters **21**

Author: Attributed to Samuel though some believe the prophets Nathan and Gad may have contributed.

Audience: Likely written during Israel's monarchy as "in those days Israel had no king" is expressed.

Setting: The Promised Land of Canaan. Difficult to date. Spans about 350 years, between 1398 & 1043 B.C. Begins with the death of Joshua, when Israel was without an earthly leader or king.

Of Interest: The time period of the judges extends into 1 Samuel.

General Information about the book of JUDGES:

After the death of Joshua, the Israelites are without a leader, everyone did what was right in their own eyes. A pattern developed which was repeated seven times in the book of Judges. The cycle began with a falling away, an enemy nation would oppress them, the Israelites called to God for deliverance, God would send a judge, the Israelites would begin a period of faith and obedience to God for a period of time before straying, and the cycle would begin again.

This repeated cycle demonstrates the faithfulness and steadfastness of God who enacts both His covenantal blessings and curses on Israel.

This book chronicles the appointments of 12 judges over a period of about 300 to 450 years. The time period dependent on the dating of the exodus from Egypt (1450 B.C. or 1290 B.C.).

The judges were: Othniel, Ehud, Shamgar, Deborah, Gideon, Tola, Jair, Jephthah, Izban, Elon, Abdon, Samson

Content Highlights:

Divided into 3 sections:
1. Introduction – the incomplete conquest of Canaan, the apostacy of Israel
2. The Judges – episodes of oppression and deliverance
3. The moral and spiritual decline of Israel

Note:
- the Judges were not magistrates or lawyers as we understand judges today but were Deliverers.
- Several judges had personal flaws, moral failures.
- Some judges may have served simultaneously, in different regions.
- Some scholars believe the content of this book is not written in chronological order.

In those days there was no king in Israel, but every man did that which was right in his own eyes.

Judges 17:6

KEY Verses:
- 2:1-4
- 2:7
- 2:10-11
- 2:18-19
- 3:1, 3-4
- 8:22-23
- 10:11-16
- 16:28-30
- 21:25

Theme: God is patient and merciful, delivering His people from their enemies.

©2023 Wildrose Media

RUTH

Literary Style: Biography

OLD Testament Book # **8** # of chapters **4**

Author: Attributed to Samuel.

Audience: Written during or shortly after the time of King David.
Written initially to the Jews but its themes and teachings are relevant for all believers.

Setting: Takes place during the time of the judges, when Israel experienced a famine.
The book begins in Moab. When Naomi's husband & sons die, she returns to Bethlehem in Judah.

Of Interest: Ruth's first husband (Naomi's deceased son) was from the tribe of Judah.
Ruth adopts Judah as her home, her descendants include King David and Jesus Christ.

General Information about the book of RUTH:

The Moabites descended from Lot, Abraham's nephew and so were (distant) blood relatives of the Israelites (see Genesis 19:36-38).

Moab was an enemy of Israel but was not included in the list of nations which God forbade the Israelites to marry. (Deut. 7:1)

The Moabites had introduced Israel to Baal worship (see Numbers 25:1-3).

Content Highlights:
- Elimelech and Naomi in Moab
- Naomi returns to Bethlehem accompanied by Ruth
- Ruth meets Boaz while gleaning in his field
- Naomi's plan
- Boaz redeems Ruth then marries her
- Birth of Obed
- Genealogy, the lineage of King David

Note:
- *Naomi* means 'pleasant'. Upon her return to Bethlehem she asked her name be changed to *Mara* which means 'bitter'.
- Ruth is one of only two books in the bible named after women (the other is Esther).
- Ruth is mentioned in the genealogy of Jesus (Matt. 1:5).

And Ruth said, "Intreat me not to leave thee, or to return from following after thee: for whither thou goest, I will go; and where thou lodgest I will lodge: thy people shall be my people, and thy God my God."

Ruth 1:16

KEY Verses:
- 1:6
- 1:16-17
- 1:20-21
- 2:1-2
- 2:11-12
- 2:19-20
- 3:114:7
- 4:9-10
- 4:17

Theme: Ruth is a story of love and redemption, foreshadowing Christ's redemption of both Jew and Gentile.

©2023 Wildrose Media

1 SAMUEL

Literary Style: Historical Narrative

OLD Testament Book # **9**   # of chapters **31**

Author: Though named for Samuel, its main character, this book's author is unknown. It is likely that several men including Samuel and the prophets Nathan and Gad contributed information, later transcribed.

Audience: Difficult to date, probably written after the death of David 971 B.C., during the divided monarchy. As a chronicle of Israel's history, written to Israel and all future Bible readers.

Setting: The events take place over about 110 years, from Israel's last judge to the death of king Saul. Takes place in the land of Israel, where God's people live among pagan people groups.

Of Interest: Samuel was a judge, but also a priest and a prophet (3:21, 7:17, 15:1, 1 Chron 6:1-2, 22-25).

General Information about the book of 1 SAMUEL:

This book marks a transition of Israel from a group of tribes to one nation under a central king.
Though Israel already had a leader, God the people insisted on an earthly king like their neighbors.
The book of First Samuel shows God's sovereignty in the world and His hand in shaping history.
It shows God's faithfulness in keeping His promises when David, from the tribe of Judah is anointed king.
It demonstrates a reversal of the expected patterns: God allows a barren woman to become a mother, He chooses both a man from Israel's lowliest tribe (Saul) and the youngest son (David) to be Israel's first kings, and He enables a young boy to slay a giant with a single stone.

Content Highlights:
- Samuel's birth and instruction under Eli the priest
- The Ark of the Covenant is captured and returned
- Samuel leads the nation of Israel
- Israel's first king, Saul
- David is anointed by Samuel as Israel's second king
- David slays Goliath, Israel's victory over the Philistines
- David in Saul's court, his friendship with Saul's son Jonathan
- David flees from Saul
- Saul's death

Note:
- 1 and 2 Samuel were originally one book. It was first divided in the Greek Septuagint.
- Samuel appointed his 2 sons to be judges, but they were dishonest and unjust men. The Israelites asked for a king rather than be led by them.

For man looketh on the outward appearance, but the Lord looketh on the heart.

1 Samuel 16:7b

KEY Verses:
- 1:11
- 1:27-28
- 2:2
- 2:10
- 2:26
- 8:6-9
- 10:1, 6-7
- 12:24-25
- 15:26-29, 35
- 16:13-14
- 24:12,13
- 28:15-19
- 29:5
- 30:6

Theme: God humbles the proud and exalts the humble.
"It is not by strength that one prevails" (vs. 9b)

©2023 Wildrose Media

2 SAMUEL

Literary Style: Historical Narrative

OLD Testament Book # **10** # of chapters **24**

Author — Though named for Samuel, this book's author is unknown. It is likely that several men including Samuel and the prophets Nathan and Gad contributed to the information found in this book.

Audience — Difficult to date, written during the divided kingdom several years after David's death (1 Sam 27:6). As a chronicle of Israel's history, written to Israel and all future Bible readers.

Setting — The events begin after the death of Saul (c. 1011 B.C.) and chronicle the 40-year reign of King David. Takes place in the land of Israel, where God's people live among pagan people groups.

Of Interest — Jesus, the Messiah is also called the son of (king) David.

General Information about the book of 2 SAMUEL:

This book demonstrates the sinfulness of man and God's mercy and forgiveness towards those who repent. Though David is known as a "man after God's own heart", he was not perfect. He was a flawed man who repeatedly sinned. When David repented, God forgave him. This remains true today. Our relationship with God can be restored when we humbly confess our sins and submit our lives to him.

God promises David's kingdom will be eternal in a covenant known as the Davidic Covenant (11:1-17). This covenant is fulfilled through the birth of Jesus Christ, David's descendant.

Content Highlights:
- David mourns for Saul and Jonathan
- David becomes King over Judah
- David becomes King over Israel, uniting the nation
- Jerusalem is established as David's capital city, brings the Ark of the Covenant there
- God establishes a covenant with David
- Battles against pagan nations
- David's adultery, the murder of Uriah, and family troubles
- The rebellion and death of Absalom and Sheba
- David's Song of Praise
- David's army, a plague, and God's forgiveness

Note
- 1 and 2 Samuel were originally one book. It was first divided in the Greek Septuagint.
- David begins his reign as king over Judah, 7 years later he is established as king over all of Israel, uniting it into one nation.
- Nathan the prophet tells David of the Covenant.

As for God, his way is perfect; the word of the Lord is tried: he is a buckler to all them that trust in Him.

2 Samuel 22:31

KEY Verses
- 1:11-12
- 3:1
- 5:1-3
- 5:9-10
- 7:12-16
- 8:15
- 12:11-13
- 21:13-14
- 22:2-4
- 22:47-51
- 24:10, 17
- 24:25

Theme — God's sovereignty and sin's consequences.

©2023 Wildrose Media

1 KINGS

Literary Style: Historical Narrative

OLD Testament Book #: 11
# of chapters: 22

Author: The authorship is unknown, some believe Ezra, Ezekiel, or Jeremiah may have contributed. It was compiled during and after the kingdom of Judah's Babylonian exile (which began c. 598 B.C.)

Audience: As a chronicle of Israel's history, 1 Kings is written to the people of Israel and all Bible readers.

Setting: Takes place in the ancient kingdoms of Israel and Judah, from about 970 B.C. to 852 B.C.

Of Interest: First and Second Kings were originally one book encompassing a time period of 400 years.

General Information about the book of 1 KINGS:

Elijah the prophet is a key figure in 1 & 2 Kings. A passionate prophet, he proclaimed God's judgement on the Israelites, confronted the prophets of Baal, and demonstrated Godly obedience to a rebellious Israel.

The divided kingdom consisted of Judah to the south and Israel to the north.

Each king of the northern or southern kingdom is evaluated for his obedience or rebellion to God's Law.

King Solomon was wise, wealthy, and well-known among other nations.

King Solomon married hundreds of foreign women in direct defiance of God's will.

In his later years, Solomon disobeys God. As a consequence, God denies Solomon's descendants the monarchy.

David's death and Solomon becomes king

Content Highlights:
- The death of King David, Solomon becomes king
- Solomon's wealth & wisdom
- Solomon builds the Temple
- The Kingdom divides
- The first kings of Judah and Israel
- Elijah the Prophet

Note:
- The Queen of Sheba may have lived in Ethiopia or modern-day Yemen.
- Elijah (spelled *Elias* in some Bible versions) means "Yahweh is my God."
- Elijah was taken up to heaven in a chariot of fire.
- During Passover, Jews set a place for Elijah at the table and leave a door open, hoping for Elijah's return. It is believed that Elijah's return signals Messiah's arrival.

And he said, LORD God of Israel, there is no God like thee, in heaven above, or on earth beneath, who keepest covenant and mercy with thy servants that walk before thee with all their heart.

1 Kings 8:23

KEY Verses:
- 1:29-30
- 2:2-4
- 2:31-33
- 3:5-14
- 4:29-34
- 6:1
- 8:10-14
- 9:3-9
- 11:9-12
- 11:34-36
- 12:20-24
- 18:36-39
- 21:25-29

Theme: God's word is true. He rewards faithfulness and punishes disobedience.

©2023 Wildrose Media

2 KINGS

Literary Style: Historical Narrative

OLD Testament Book # **12** # of chapters **25**

Author > The authorship is unknown, some believe Ezra, Ezekiel, or Jeremiah may have contributed. It was compiled from eyewitness sources during the Babylonian exile, between c. 561-538 B.C.

Audience > As a chronicle of Israel's history, written to Israel and all future Bible readers.

Setting > Takes place in from about 852 B.C. to 561 B.C. Events occur in the land of Israel, from Dan to Beersheba.

Of Interest > Daniel was among those captured and sent to Babylon.

General Information about the book of 2 KINGS:

2 Kings continues the saga of the divided kingdom, Judah to the south and Israel to the north. Both kingdoms have turned from God, and except for an occasional obedient king, they worship pagan gods.
As promised by God, the nation's disobedience and rebellion results in punishment.
The nations are captured and live in exile.
In 1 Kings Elijah names Elisha as his successor. After Elijah is taken to heaven, Elisha bears the responsibility to bring God's word and warnings to the northern kingdom for more than 50 years. He died of an illness.
The kingdom of Israel was conquered by the Assyrians in 722 B.C.
In 586 B.C. the Babylonians invade Judah, destroying Jerusalem and the Temple.

Content Highlights:
- Elijah taken up to heaven
- Elisha and the Northern Kingdom
- A History of the Kings of Israel and Judah
- The exile of Israel (Northern Kingdom)
- King Josiah and the Temple
- The fall and exile of Judah (northern Kingdom)

- All the kings of Israel (the northern kingdom) and most of the kings of Judah (the southern kingdom) "did evil in the sight of the Lord". **Note**
- God sends prophets to warn His people, to encourage them to turn from their idolatry and wicked ways.
- Israel's continued rejection of God, despite these warnings result in destruction of their nation and the exile of Judah.

And it came to pass, as they still went on, and talked, that, behold, there appeared a chariot of fire, and horses of fire, and parted them both asunder; and Elijah went up by a whirlwind into heaven.

2 Kings 2:11

KEY Verses
- 2:11, 15
- 4:1-7
- 6:15-17
- 8:11-13
- 8:16-19
- 12:1-5
- 17:5-8
- 18:1-5
- 23:1-3
- 23:26-27
- 24:20
- 25:8-12

Theme > Rebellion against God results in punishment.

©2023 Wildrose Media

1 CHRONICLES

Literary Style: Historical Narrative

OLD Testament Book # **13**   # of chapters **29**

Author → Author is unknown. Jewish tradition gives Ezra credit. It was likely written between 583- 333 B.C. Ch. 29:29 references the annals of Samuel, Nathan, and Gad which may have been consulted.

Audience → Written to the exiles who returned to Israel after the Babylonian captivity.

Setting → Events occur in the Promised Land of Canaan, the nation of Israel from c. 1011 B.C. to c. 971 B.C. Begins with a genealogy of the Jews from Adam to Saul, ends with King David's death.

Of Interest → Jerome's Latin Vulgate (c. A.D. 400) used the title *The Chronicles of the Entire Sacred History*.

General Information about the book of 1 CHRONICLES:
1 & 2 Chronicles cover the same time period as 1 & 2 Samuel and 1 & 2 Kings but offer additional information. It provides a chronicle of God's work of redemption in His people and points us to Christ, the true King. The Jews in exile can have hope because of God's promise to David of a future, everlasting Kingdom.

Content Highlights:
- Genealogy from Adam to Saul
- The death of King Saul
- King David
- God's covenant with David
- Battles Fought
- Preparations for the Temple in Jerusalem
- The Levites
- Solomon becomes king
- The death of King David

Note ←
- The book (a single book until c. A.D. 200) of Chronicles is referred to in 1st & 2nd Kings as the *Annals of the Kings of Israel* (10:34)
- The original title in the Hebrew bible was the *Annals of the Days*.
- In the original Jewish bible, Chronicles is the last book of the Old Testament

O give thanks unto the Lord; for he is good; for his mercy endureth forever.

1 Chronicles 16:34

KEY Verses ↓
- 10:13-14
- 16:8
- 16:22
- 17:14
- 17:20-22
- 22:6-10
- 22:19
- 28:20
- 29:14
- 29:18-20

Theme → A reminder to be faithful to God and His covenant, as God is faithful.

©2023 Wildrose Media

2 CHRONICLES

Literary Style: Historical Narrative

OLD Testament Book #: **14**

# of chapters: **36**

Author: Jewish tradition attributes this book to Ezra.

Audience: Originally written to the ancient Jews but is for all readers of the bible. Written c. 430 B.C.

Setting: Events occur in Judah, the Southern Kingdom from c. 971 B.C. to c. 538 B.C. Begins with Solomon's reign and ends with King Cyrus allowing the exiles to return to Jerusalem.

Of Interest: Jerome's Latin Vulgate (c. A.D. 400) used the title *The Chronicles of the Entire Sacred History*.

General Information about the book of 2 CHRONICLES:

1 & 2 Chronicles cover the same time period as 1 & 2 Samuel and 1 & 2 Kings but offer additional information.
It provides a chronicle of God's work of redemption in His people and points us to Christ, the true King.
The Jews in exile can have hope because of God's promise to David of an everlasting Kingdom.
This book describes the evil kings of Judah briefly, focusing instead on the kings which feared & obeyed God.
Parallels for the building of both the tabernacle (see Exodus) and the Temple are notable, details which are not in either Samuel or Kings.

Content Highlights:
- The reign of King Solomon
- Solomon builds the Temple
- The nation of Israel is divided
- The Kings of Judah
- The fall of Jerusalem & exile into Babylon
- The completion of Judah's 70-year captivity in Persia

Note:
- The four books of 1st & 2nd Chronicles, Ezra, and Nehemiah form a four-book series.
- The last words of 2nd Chronicles are the first words of Ezra.

But they mocked the messengers of God, and despised his words, and misused his prophets until the wrath of the Lord arose against his people, till there was no remedy.

2 Chronicles 36:16

KEY Verses:
- 1:8-12
- 2:5
- 5:13-6:2
- 6:14-17
- 7:1-3
- 7:14
- 11:13-17
- 13:12
- 19:6,9
- 20:21-22
- 21:29
- 24:20
- 28:24-25
- 30:6-13
- 33:10-12,16
- 36:15-19
- 36:22-23

Theme: Restoration. God is a God of love and forgiveness.

©2023 Wildrose Media

EZRA

Literary Style: Historical Narrative

OLD Testament Book #: **15**

# of chapters: **10**

Author > Likely Ezra. Most scholars agree the author(s) of 1 & 2 Chronicles also wrote Ezra & Nehemiah. Written around 440 B.C., shortly after Nehemiah's ministry.

Audience > Written to the Jews and to all future bible readers.

Setting > Takes place between 539-458 B.C. Begins in Babylon, ends in Jerusalem, Judah.

Of Interest > The concluding verses of 2 Chronicles are almost identical to the opening words of Ezra.

General Information about the book of EZRA:

The Persians conquered the Babylonians in 539 B.C.
After 70 years in captivity Persian King Cyrus allowed the Jews to return to Judah and rebuild the Temple.
The Temple reconstruction was begun in 536 B.C. and completed in 515 B.C.
Ezra arrived in Jerusalem in 458 B.C., after the Temple was rebuilt.
He led the second group of returning exiles.
Ezra was a Levite priest from the line of Aaron (see 7:1-6).
He taught the Jews the Law and supervised the reestablishment of sacrifices and feast days.

Content Highlights:
- The return of the first exiles to Judah.
- Interference of rival nations.
- The Temple is rebuilt.
- Ezra returns to Jerusalem with the second group of exiles.

- The name *Ezra* means 'YAHWEH helps'
- Parts of this book are written in Aramaic

Note

The hand of our God is upon all them for good that seek him; but his power and his wrath is against all them that forsake him.

Ezra 8:22b

KEY Verses
- 1:1-3
- 1:7
- 2:68-70
- 3:10-13
- 4:4-5
- 6:21-22
- 7:1,6,10
- 7:13, 25-26
- 8:21-23
- 8:28-30
- 10:2-3
- 10:16-17

Theme > God's grace and continuing covenant with Israel.

©2023 Wildrose Media

NEHEMIAH

Literary Style: Historical Narrative

OLD Testament Book # **16** # of chapters **13**

Author → Most scholars agree the author(s) of 1 & 2 Chronicles also wrote Ezra & Nehemiah. As priest & scribe Ezra had access to the royal archives in Persia.

Audience → The Jewish people and all bible readers.

Setting → Begins in Persia, then to Israel after Nehemiah travels to Jerusalem in 444 B.C. Is an account of Nehemiah's complete first term and partial second term as governor.

Of Interest → Nehemiah was cupbearer to King Artaxerxes; he gave it up to become governor of Jerusalem. He was governor for 2 terms, from 445-433 B.C. and again from c. 424 - 410 B.C.

General Information about the book of NEHEMIAH:

Nehemiah returned to Judah to help rebuild the wall around Jerusalem. The wall was completed in 52 days.
He was part of the third group of exiles to return to Judah.
Nehemiah 1-12 covers a timespan of about 1 year, chapter 13 begins 20 years later.
Together Ezra and Nehemiah work to restore the practical and spiritual lives of God's people.

Content Highlights:

- Nehemiah hears of Jerusalem's troubles and prays
- Nehemiah returns to Jerusalem to rebuild the walls
- The wall is completed
- The people who returned to Judah are registered
- Renewal of the Covenant
- The Feast of Tabernacles
- Nehemiah goes to Persia
- The wall is dedicated
- Nehemiah returns to Jerusalem for a second term as governor

Then I answered them, and said unto them, "the God of heaven, he will prosper us; therefore we his servants will arise and build..."

Nehemiah 2:20a

- The name Nehemiah means *Jehovah comforts*.
- Both the Septuagint and the Latin Vulgate named this book *Second Ezra*.

Note

KEY Verses

- 1:3-7
- 2:17-18
- 4:14
- 5:9-13
- 5:14
- 5:19
- 6:15-16
- 8:2-3, 6
- 9:5b-6
- 9:32-33

Theme → Restoration. God's covenant faithfulness to Israel.

©2023 Wildrose Media

ESTHER

Literary Style: Biography

OLD Testament Book # **17**   # of chapters **10**

Author: Unknown for certain. The author was familiar with both Persian and Jewish customs and Feasts..

Audience: Written to the ancient Jews and to all bible readers.

Setting: The book of Esther takes place in Susa, Persia from 483-473 B.C., during the time of King Xerxes. It occurs about 25 years before Ezra leads the second group of exiles to Jerusalem.

Of Interest: There is no direct mention of God and His name does not appear in this book. The Jews read the book of Esther and celebrate God's deliverance each year during Purim.

General Information about the book of ESTHER:
- Esther's Hebrew name was Hadassah
- Esther was an orphan, raised in Persia by her cousin Mordecai
- After Queen Vashti was banished due to her disobedience, a kingdom-wide search for her replacement occurred
- Esther was brought into the palace at Susa as part of the king's harem and was treated very well.
- Esther was made queen of Persia in 473 B.C.
- The animosity between Haman and Mordecai stemmed from their ancestral roots. Haman was from the Amalekite nation, sworn enemies of the Jews.

Content Highlights:
- Queen Vashti is deposed at the King's banquet
- Esther becomes Queen
- Haman's plot to destroy the Jews
- Mordecai asks Esther for help
- Haman is executed
- Victory for the Jews
- Purim is celebrated

Then Esther the queen answered and said, If I have found favor in thy sight, O king, and if it please the king, let my life be given me at my petition, and my people at my request.

Esther 7:3

Note:
- The Jews celebrate two annual festivals which were not part of the Mosaic Law, the Feast of Purim and the Festival of Lights.
- Esther is the Old Testament's last recorded attempt of eradicating God's people.

KEY Verses:
- 1:10, 12
- 2:1-4
- 2:7-10
- 2:17
- 3:5-11
- 4:15-16
- 7:1-10
- 8:11
- 9:27-28

Theme: God is faithful, He preserves His people.

©2023 Wildrose Media

JOB

Literary Style: Poetry, Wisdom Literature

OLD Testament Book #: **18** | # of chapters: **42**

Author: Unknown, though some attribute it to Moses.

Audience: All readers of the Bible, possibly originally written to the enslaved Hebrews in Egypt.

Setting: Events in Job seem to have occurred after Babel but before Abraham. The Prologue is a dialogue between God and Satan in heaven. Job lived in the land of Uz.

Of Interest: Satan must ask permission from God to test Job. Satan means *the accuser*.

General Information about the book of JOB:

Job is the account of a wealthy, faithful man, who is tested by Satan.
God's character is revealed.
The first chapter sets the scene and explains the premise for the book.
Satan questions Job's motives for loving and serving God and seeks to prove Job is doing it to get rewarded
Despite losing his children, his riches, his home, his wife, and his health Job refuses to curse God.

Content Highlights:
- Introduction to Job
- Satan approaches God in heaven
- Job's first test
- Job's second test
- Dialogue between Job and his three friends
- God speaks to Job
- God rebukes Job's friends
- God blesses Job

All the while my breath is in me, and the spirit of God is in my nostrils; My lips shall not speak wickedness, nor my tongue utter deceit.

Job 27:3-4

Note:
- Several clues in the book of Job date it to the time of the patriarchs: his long lifespan, no mention of the Mosaic law, and offering sacrifices himself, wealth measured in livestock.
- It is speculated that the land of Uz was in northern Arabia

KEY Verses:
- 1:8
- 1:12
- 1:20-21
- 2:9-10
- 5:17
- 11:7
- 12:10, 13, 16
- 19:25-27
- 23:13-14
- 27:3-4
- 42:1-6
- 42:10

Theme: God as the authority over all, trust Him despite our circumstances.

©2023 Wildrose Media

THE BOOK OF PSALMS

Literary Style: Poetry, Songs of Praise, Wisdom

OLD Testament Book # **19** # of chapters **150**

Author: David wrote about 73 psalms. Other psalmists were the sons of Asaph (12) and Korah (11), David's son Solomon (2), Moses (1), "Orphans" (50), and the Ezrahites - brothers Ethan (1) and Heman (1).

Audience: The ancient Hebrews and all readers of the Bible. This book is categorized as a book of Wisdom in the Bible.

Setting: Though difficult to date, the Psalms were likely written over 1000 years between 1500 to 500 B.C. The Psalms were probably compiled into one book in the 3rd century B.C.

Of Interest: The ancient Hebrew title for this book is *Tehillim*, meaning 'Praises'. Asaph and his family were worship leaders under David, later recommissioned by Nehemiah.

General Information about the book of PSALMS:

The Psalms are lyric poems, many of which were set to music and used in public worship.
The Psalms were divided into 5 books as follows: 1 (#1-41), 2 (#42-72), 3 (#73-89), 4 (#90-106), 5 (#107-150).
Many emotions are expressed in this book- including anger, despair, joy, praise, and humility.
The authors used literary devices such as repetition, assonance, alliteration, characterization, similes, and metaphors in their poems.
The word Selah is found 71 times in 39 Psalms, it is uncertain what this word means. It is thought to be related to instrumentation or musical accompaniment.

Content Highlights:

- There are several themes or types of Psalms. Some Psalms may fit into more than one themed category.
- Historical Psalms – God's acts and Israel's response
- Psalms of Praise and Adoration to God
- Psalms of Lament
- Psalms of Thanksgiving
- Liturgical Psalms – worship, used during Feasts
- Imprecatory/Petition – call on God for help
- Relational Psalms – between God and writer
- Prophetic Psalms – coming Messiah

Note:
- Unlike the rest of the Bible the chapter headings were included in the ancient manuscripts.
- The Hebrew word for Psalm, *mizmôr* means 'melody'. Mizmôr was translated as *psalmos* in the Greek Septuagint.
- Many consider Psalms the longest book in the Bible as it has the most chapters, but Jeremiah and Genesis have more words (in the original languages).

Let the words of my mouth, and the meditation of my heart, be acceptable in thy sight, O LORD, my strength, and my redeemer.

Psalm 19:14

KEY Verses:
- Psalm 1
- Psalm 8
- Psalm 14:1
- Psalm 15
- Psalm 19
- Psalm 23
- Psalm 27:4
- Psalm 46:1
- Psalm 51:10
- Psalm 55
- Psalm 62
- Psalm 91
- Psalm 96
- Psalm 100
- Psalm 103
- Psalm 119:105
- Psalm 121
- Psalm 139

Theme: God is the sovereign center of life, history, and the universe. He deserves our worship.

©2023 Wildrose Media

PROVERBS

Literary Style: Poetry, Wisdom Literature

OLD Testament Book # **20** # of chapters **31**

Author: Known authors are King Solomon, King Hezekiah, Lemuel, and Agur. Several proverbs, referred to as the "sayings of the wise" are of unknown authorship, likely written prior to Solomon.

Audience: Youth ("my son"), men and women, all readers of the Bible.
Purpose is to guide readers in making wise, just, and righteous decisions.

Setting: Solomon ruled Israel from 971- 931 B.C. Hezekiah ruled Judah from c. 715-686 B.C.

Of Interest: Several of these proverbs are similar to Egyptian and Mesopotamian proverbs.
Chapter 31 offers attributes of an ideal wife – godly, diligent, gracious, and creative.

General Information about the book of PROVERBS:

Proverbs are simple, moral statements which give practical advice on Godly living.
The Proverbs are not all absolute truths, also included are guidelines and principles for godly living, and observations of how the world works.
These sayings remain applicable to our lives today.
There is no plot or storyline in the book of Proverbs.
It is a collection of sayings which address many opposing topics, including wisdom and foolishness, joy vs. anger, diligence vs. laziness, justice vs. injustice, what God loves vs. what He hates.

Content Highlights:

Much of the content is presented as a teacher addressing a student or a parent, his child.
The book of Proverbs includes:
- Instructions and arguments for wisdom vs. foolishness
- Two-line sayings which are easy to remember and apply
- Acrostics – the first word of each sentence form a word
- Other sayings (longer than two lines)

Note:
- A proverb is a figure of speech which allows a person to express complex ideas in a compact statement. It is often culturally or traditionally based and may be down passed from generation to generation.
- Proverbs often educate or offer advice, wisdom, and moral truths.

The fear of the LORD is the beginning of knowledge: but fools despise wisdom and instruction.

Proverbs 1:7

KEY Verses:
- 1:32-33
- 3:5-6
- 6:16-19
- 8:36
- 9:10
- 10:11
- 13:1, 3
- 14:16, 31
- 15:1, 28
- 18:12, 21
- 21:3
- 26:28
- 28:6
- 29:23
- 31:10-31

Theme: True wisdom comes from God.

©2023 Wildrose Media

ECCLESIASTES

Literary Style: Poetry

OLD Testament Book #: 21
# of chapters: 12

Author: The author is unknown but identifies himself as a teacher. Some believe it may have been Solomon as the book gives clues such as wealth, wisdom, descendent of David which suggest this may be true.

Audience: Written to offer wisdom to the Jewish people and all readers of the Bible.

Setting: No time period is mentioned, but if written by Solomon it is dated between 970-931 B.C. The nation of Israel at the end of the Persian Period.

Of Interest: The title means 'Gatherer, Teacher, or Preacher'. The book *Ecclesiasticus* is an apocryphal book written by Jesus Sirach.

General Information about the book of ECCLESIASTES:

Ecclesiastes belongs to the category of Wisdom Literature.
Deals with the meaning of life.
The author makes the point that life is meaningless apart from God.
Vanities are mentioned frequently in this book. Vanities are pointless, empty, or futile human activities which have short-lived, if any benefits.

Content Highlights:
- Preface
- Introduction
- Seeking Meaning Through Pleasure
- Seeking Meaning Through Wisdom and Folly
- Seeking Wisdom Through Work and Rewards
- Conclusions - Man's Limitations and Human Mortality
- Words of Advice
- Information About the Author

Fear God, and keep his commandments: for this is the whole duty of man. For God shall bring every work into judgment, with every secret thing whether it be good or whether it be evil.

Ecclesiastes 12:13b-14

Note:
- In the Jewish Bible (the Tanakh) Ecclesiastes is part of the section called *Ketuvim* (Writings). It is part of the *Megillot,* 5 scrolls which are grouped together and read at Feast days.
- Included in the 5 scrolls are the books of Ruth, Lamentations, Esther, Song of Songs, and Ecclesiastes.

KEY Verses
- 1:2, 8-11
- 1:18
- 2:12-14
- 3:1-8
- 3:14
- 4:9-12
- 5:5
- 5:12
- 5:19
- 7:14
- 11:5
- 12:13-14

Theme: Without God, life is meaningless.

©2023 Wildrose Media

SONG OF SONGS

Literary Style: Poetry

OLD Testament Book # **22** # of chapters **8**

Author: King Solomon (1:1).
Written over a period of about 1-2 years.

Audience: A love poem written between Solomon and a Shulamite woman.

Setting: Written during the reign of Israel's King Solomon, from c. 971 – 931 B.C.

Of Interest: This book does not mention God or claim to present a specific message from Him.
This book is sometimes called *The Song of Solomon* or *Canticle of Canticles*.

General Information about the book of SONG of SONGS:

In the Writings, Song of Songs is included as a Wisdom Book in Hebrew scripture. It is one of the 5 scrolls of the Megillot and is typically read during the Feast of Pesach (Passover).

A love song which celebrates and illustrates ideal love between man and wife.

This poem is written with 3 voices – the lover, the beloved, and "friends".

The authors use similes from nature to express the lovers' passion for one another.

Content Highlights:
- Courtship and Expression of Longing
- Praise of the Beloved
- Praises of the Bride
- Disappearance of the Lover
- The Lovers are Reunited

Note:
- Scholars, both Jewish and Christian have made parallels between this book and God's love for Israel or Jesus' love for the Church.
- King Solomon eventually had 700 wives and 300 concubines, leading some to doubt his authorship.

I am my beloved's, and his desire is toward me.

Song of Songs 7:10

KEY Verses:
- 1:2
- 1:15-16
- 2:2
- 2:5
- 2:12
- 2:16
- 3:4-5
- 4:9
- 5:8
- 7:9
- 7:12
- 8:6

Theme: A celebration of God-ordained intimacy between man and wife.

©2023 Wildrose Media

ISAIAH

Literary Style: Prose, Poetry, Prophecy

OLD Testament Book # **23** | # of chapters **66**

Author → The prophet Isaiah.
Isaiah was a gifted writer, used literary techniques including imagery, personification, and metaphors.

Audience → God used Isaiah to speak His message to the people of Judah.

Setting → Event occur in the southern kingdom of Judah, specifically in and around Jerusalem.
Isaiah ministered during four kings – Uzziah, Jotham, Ahaz, & Hezekiah (c. 739-686 B.C.)

Of Interest → The people of Israel and Judah rarely listened to the prophets.
Isaiah wrote a biography of King Hezekiah (Chronicles 32:32).

General Information about the book of ISAIAH:

Is one of the Major Prophets.
It is called the 'book of salvation" as many of Isaiah's prophecies concern Jesus, the Messiah.
Has the clearest statements about the gospel in the Old Testament, written 700 years before the Savior's birth.
These prophesies cover the announcement of his coming, Jesus' virgin birth, His ministry, His death, His return.
There is division among the church regarding the prophetic references to Israel, some believe the church has replaced Israel while others maintain ethnic Israel will receive these promises.
Isaiah uses the title "The Holy One of Israel" 25 times, referring to God.

Content Highlights:

Chapters 1-35	Messages of Judgment Against Judah
	A Call to Repentance and Holiness
	Promised Restoration
Chapters 36-39	Isaiah's Ministry to Hezekiah
Chapters 40-66	Messages of Forgiveness, Comfort, Hope, and Salvation
	The Future Messiah
	The Future Kingdom

Note:
- The name *Isaiah* means "the Lord is salvation".
- The book of Isaiah is quoted 66 times in the NT, more than any OT prophet. (Only the Psalms are quoted more).
- Isaiah was a contemporary of the prophets Amos, Hosea, and Micah.
- Tradition holds that Isaiah was killed (sawed in half) by king Manasseh.

Behold, God is my salvation; I will trust, and not be afraid: for the LORD JEHOVAH is my strength and my song; he also is become my salvation.

Isaiah 12:2

KEY Verses:
- 1:16-20
- Ch. 6
- 7:14
- 9:2-7
- Ch. 11
- 12:2
- 14:12-15
- Ch. 24
- Ch. 26+27
- Ch. 34+35
- Ch. 40
- 41:10
- 45:7
- Ch. 53
- 54:17
- 55:6-9
- 55:6-9
- 57:1-2
- 60:1
- 64:6, 8-9
- Ch. 65+66

Theme → God's plan for the world, and He is the source of salvation.

©2023 Wildrose Media

JEREMIAH

Literary Style: Anthology, Prophecy, Poetry

OLD Testament Book # **24** # of chapters **52**

Author: Jeremiah, prophet and son of a priest, Hilkiah. He was chosen by God before birth (1:4-5). Baruch and Seraiah wrote Jeremiah's prophecies on a scroll (ch. 36 & 51).

Audience: The Israelites in Judah, and all future readers of the Bible.

Setting: Southern kingdom of Judah, during the reign of Kings Josiah, Jehoiakim, Jehoiachin, and Zedekiah. Jeremiah served as prophet from about 627 B.C. to after 586 B.C. (the fall of Jerusalem).

Of Interest: Jeremiah is the longest prophetic book in the Bible. It was written circa 586 - 570 B.C.

General Information about the book of JEREMIAH:
It is a collection, or anthology of prophetic sermons preached over more than 20 years.
Jeremiah prophesied the destruction of Jerusalem and lived to see this prophecy fulfilled.
Jeremiah repeatedly calls for repentance and criticizes Judah's kings. For this he endured many trials, including being beaten (20:2), seized (26:8 & 37:21), thrown in a cistern & starved (38:1-13), rejected.
Jeremiah was instructed not to participate in society, feast days and was not permitted to marry (16:2, 5, 8), to place a yoke around his neck (27:1-11)
This book is not written in chronological order.

Content Highlights:
Chapter 1-29 God's call to Jeremiah and Jeremiah's prophecies against Judah
    God pronounces judgment on Judah for idolatry, breaking the covenant.
Chapter 7-10 The Temple Sermon
Chapter 25 God's wrath extends to all nations (25:19-26)
Chapter 30-33 Restoration and the New Covenant
Chapter 46-49 Prophesies of judgment against the nations
Chapter 50-51 The Babylonians, having been used by God to punish Israel, must now pay for their wickedness
Chapter 34-39, 52 The Fall of Jerusalem

But this shall be the covenant that I will make with the house of Israel; After those days, saith the LORD, I will put my law in their inward parts, and write it in their hearts; and will be their God, and they shall be my people.

Jeremiah 31:33

Note:
- The prophets Zephaniah, Habakkuk, Ezekiel, and Daniel are Jeremiah's contemporaries.
- Chaldean tribes control Babylonia by the 7th century BC, these terms are used interchangeably in the Bible.

KEY Verses:
- 1:9-10, 14
- 5:14-18
- 9:23-24
- 13:11
- 16:14-15
- 22:8-9
- 23:5-6, 20
- 26:16-19
- 31:29-30
- 31:31-34
- 33: 14-22
- 46:28
- 51:47-49
- Chapter 52

Theme: Judgment and hope. God punishes sin, but remains steadfast and faithful.

©2023 Wildrose Media

LAMENTATIONS

Literary Style: Poetry

OLD Testament Book # **25** # of chapters **5**

Author › Author is not named in the book but both Jewish and Christian tradition believe Jeremiah wrote it. Jeremiah is known as 'the weeping prophet'.

Audience › The captured Israelites and all future readers of the Bible.

Setting › Written after the destruction of Jerusalem by the Babylonians which occurred in 586 B.C. Jeremiah may have written it after his journey from Egypt to Babylon.

Of Interest › In chapters 1-4 the first letter of each verse forms an acrostic of the Hebrew alphabet. Each of the 22 letters in the Hebrew alphabet are present, in order. Chapter 5 has 22 verses.

General Information about the book of LAMENTATIONS:

The title means *funeral songs,* an expression of great sorrow or mourning.
The book begins with the author asking, "How could this happen?"
The people of Israel had repeatedly broken their promise to love and obey God and instead rejected Him. God, though patient and merciful, is also just. He could not let their disobedience remain unpunished. Jerusalem is destroyed, and the people captured but hope remains for their future redemption.

Content Highlights:
Consists of 5 poems, one per chapter.
1. Jerusalem's Destruction
2. God's Anger and Punishment
3. Jeremiah's Grief, a Personal Experience
4. God's Wrath
5. Prayer for God's Mercy

Turn thou us unto thee, O Lord, and we shall be turned; renew our days as of old.

Lamentations 5:21

- One of the 5 Scrolls, also known as the *Ketuvim* (Writings) or *Megillot*.
- Lamentations is read on the 9th of Av, an annual day of fasting and mourning (Tisha B'Av) which commemorates the destruction of the Temple in Jerusalem by the Babylonians in 586 B.C., and the Romans in AD 70.

Note

KEY Verses

- 1:1, 5
- 1:8
- 2:17
- 3:19-26
- 3:31-33
- 3:37-39
- 4:22
- 5:15-16
- 5:19-21

Theme › God is faithful, merciful, and just. He fulfills his covenant promises. God rewards the faithful and disciplines the unfaithful.

©2023 Wildrose Media

EZEKIEL

Literary Style: Allegory, History, Prophecy

OLD Testament Book #: **26**
# of chapters: **48**

Author: The prophet Ezekiel, who was from a priestly family. He was called to preach a message of God's judgment and the restoration of Israel.

Audience: The Israeli exiles in Babylon, the Jews remaining in Judea, and all future readers of the Bible.

Setting: Ezekiel ministered to the community of exiles living in Babylon. The book begins around 593 B.C., 5 years after the exile, then continues 22 years later - in 571 B.C.

Of Interest: The book of Ezekiel is precise, contains more dates than any other Old Testament prophetic book. Ezekiel provides a detailed description of Cherubim (ch. 1 &10).

General Information about the book of EZEKIEL:

Ezekiel writes in parables, allegories, and has several visions or *oracles* (wise and insightful counsel or prophetic predictions) from the Lord which he describes in this book.

Ezekiel was married, his wife died but God did not allow him to mourn her. This was a sign for Israel not to mourn Jerusalem.

The global church differs in its eschatological (end times) views, and there are four main beliefs about the meaning of Ezekiel's prophecies, based on whether one uses a literal or a figurative interpretation, and ascribe to a covenantal or dispensationalist view. These debated references include the Battle of Armageddon, Gog and Magog, and especially the Temple.

Content Highlights:

Chapters 1-3 Ezekiel's Commission
Chapters 4-24 God's Judgment on Jerusalem and Judah
Chapters 8-11 Temple Vision, God's Glory Departs
Chapters 25-32 Oracles of God's Judgment Against Foreign Nations
Chapter 33 The Fall of Jerusalem & Captivity
Chapter 37 Valley of Dry Bones
Chapters 33-40 Future Blessings, The Restoration of Israel and Judah
Chapters 40-46 Israel and the New Temple

Note:
- The prophesies of Ezekiel are seen in visions by John, which he describes in the book of Revelation.
- The OT has four separate accounts of the fall of Jerusalem (in Chronicles, 2 Kings, Jeremiah, and Ezekiel).

A new heart also will I give you, and a new spirit will I put within you: and I will take away the stony heart out of your flesh, and I will give you a heart of flesh.

Ezekiel 36:26

KEY Verses:
- 2:1-7
- 3:10-11
- 5:5-8
- 5:11-15
- 6:8-10
- 11:16-21
- 12:28
- 16:59-60
- 18:1-4, 20
- 18:30-32
- 34:17, 22-31
- 36:22-27
- 37:1-14
- 37:26-28
- 39:21-22
- 43:7
- 44:15-16
- 47:21-23

Theme: God's sovereignty. He is holy and must be honored.

©2023 Wildrose Media

DANIEL

Literary Style: Prophecy

OLD Testament Book # **27** | # of chapters **12**

Author: Daniel was among the first group of Jews brought to captivity in Babylon by King Nebuchadnezzar II.

Audience: Written to encourage the exiled Jews. Daniel contains end-times prophecy. Much of Daniel was written in Aramaic, the language of international business.

Setting: Events take place between 605 and 535 B.C. during Judah's Babylonian captivity.

Of Interest: Ch 10 describes an ongoing spiritual battle for the nations which occurs between demons & angels. Art often depicts him as a young man, but Daniel was about 80 when thrown into the lion's den.

General Information about the book of DANIEL:

Daniel and his friends were chosen to serve in to serve in the King's palace for their good looks and intellect.
God blessed them with wisdom and health, for they obeyed God's law despite their new circumstances.
Nine of the twelve chapters contain revelations in the form of dream or visions.
God enables Daniel to interpret dreams and visions.
The Hebrew canon considers Daniel a historical book, not prophetic. Daniel did not call Israel to repentance.

Content Highlights:

Chapter 1 Daniel and his friends are faithful in captivity.
Chapter 2 Nebuchadnezzar II Dreams of a Statue, Daniel interprets it.
Chapter 3 The Fiery Furnace
Chapter 4 Nebuchadnezzar II's Dream of the Tall Tree, Daniel interprets it.
Chapter 5 The Writing on the Wall, and Daniels interpretation. Darius becomes king over Babylon.
Chapter 6 Daniel in the Lion's Den
Chapter 7 & 8 Daniel's Vision of Four Beasts, (representing world kingdoms), the Antichrist, and Tribulation.
Chapter 9 Daniel's Prayer, Prophecy of the 70 Weeks
Chapter 10-12 Vision of the Future - End Times, the Kings of the North and South.

Note: The four young men were renamed by Nebuchadnezzar II:
- Daniel became Belteshazzar (Bel will protect)
- Hananiah became Shadrach (inspired of Aku)
- Mishael became Meshach (belonging to Aku)
- Azariah became Abednego (servant of Nego)

Note: Bel (Ba'al) was the chief god, god of fertility
Aku was a moon-god
Nego was the god of wisdom

"... for he is the living God, and stedfast for ever, and his kingdom that which shall not be destroyed, and his dominion shall be even unto the end".

Daniel 6:27b

KEY Verses

- 2:19-23
- 2:27-30
- 2:31-49
- 3:17-30
- 3:34
- 4:37
- 5:21
- 6:25-27
- 7:13-14
- 7:23-27
- 8:13-14
- 9:17-27
- 10:10-14
- 11:40-45
- 12:1-2, 9-12

Theme: 1. Hope for Israel's future. 2. God's sovereignty over all nations.

©2023 Wildrose Media

HOSEA

Literary Style: Poetry, Prose, History & Prophecy

OLD Testament Book # **28** # of chapters **14**

Author: Written by Hosea, one of the 12 minor prophets.

Audience: The people of the Northern Kingdom of Israel and of Judah, and all future readers of the Bible. His focus was the Northern Kingdom, it is mentioned by name 81 times, but Judah only 15 times.

Setting: Hosea was a prophet born in the Northern Kingdom, which he calls Ephraim. He ministered in Israel and Judah from c. 755 - 715 B.C. and was a contemporary of the prophets Micah and Isaiah.

Of Interest: The name *Hosea* means 'salvation'. Hosea is known as the 'gentle prophet'.

General Information about the book of HOSEA:

Hosea married a woman who became unfaithful to him. Several times she broke their marriage covenant and sought after other men. Each time Hosea forgave her, even rescuing her from slavery.

Hosea's experience reflects God's pain when His people turn from Him.

God names the couple's three children. Each name is a message from God for the people of Israel and Judah.

Hosea's love for his unfaithful wife, Gomer mirrors God's love for His wayward people, Israel.

Hosea prophesied about Assyria's invasion of Israel as punishment for their idolatry and wicked ways.

Depicts God as a loving husband and father, a physician, and a fruit-bearing tree. He is able to fulfill our needs.

Content Highlights:

- Hosea's Marriage and Children
- Israel's Sin
- Hosea's Message for Israel
- God's Discipline
- God's Merciful Restoration
- Hosea lives to see his prophecy of captivity transpire when the Northern Kingdom is conquered by Assyria.

...for the ways of the Lord are right; and the just shall walk in them: but the transgressors shall fall therein.

Hosea 14:9b

KEY Verses:
- 2:8
- 2:18-20
- 3:1
- 3:4
- 4:1
- 5:14-15
- 6:1
- 6:6
- 7:13-15
- 9:1-3
- 9:17
- 12:6
- 13:4-5

Theme: God's enduring love and faithfulness to His people, despite their idolatry.

©2023 Wildrose Media

JOEL

Literary Style: Poetry, Prophecy

OLD Testament Book #: 29
# of chapters: 3

Author: The prophet Joel (1:1).
This is book 2 of the minor prophets.

Audience: The Jews living in Judah during the reign of King Joash and all readers of the Bible.

Setting: About 250 years before the Babylonian exile (586 B.C.).
In the Southern Kingdom of Judah, likely during King Joash's reign, c.835 – 796 B.C.

Of Interest: Joel was a contemporary of the prophet Elisha.

General Information about the book of JOEL:

Two speeches – God's judgement and God's mercy.
Three main sections.
- God wants Judah to repent. He sent a plague of locusts as punishment for their unfaithfulness.
- God promises to bless Judah and restore His covenant with them when they repent.
- God will one day judge all nations.

Content Highlights:
- A Plague of Locusts (either real or symbolic)
- A Call for Repentance
- The Day of the Lord
- A Call for Repentance
- The Lord's Final Judgment on the Nations
- Restoration and Blessings for God's People

Note:
- The promise of Joel 3:1-5 is seen at Pentecost, Acts 2:16-21. God pours out His Spirit into the hearts of His people.

And rend your heart, and not your garments, and turn unto the LORD your God: for he is gracious and merciful, slow to anger, and of great kindness, and repenteth him of the evil.

Joel 2:13

KEY Verses:
- 1:15
- 2:1-2
- 2:11-13
- 2:18
- 2:27
- 2:28-32
- 3:17, 20-21

Theme: Be prepared, the Day of the Lord is near.

©2023 Wildrose Media

AMOS

Literary Style: Narrative, Exhortation, Poetry

OLD Testament Book #: **30**
# of chapters: **9**

Author: Amos, a shepherd from a village south of Jerusalem. He was called to be a prophet in Israel. (7:14-15).

Audience: Amos ministered to the Jews in the Northern Kingdom. This book was written to them and all readers of the Bible.

Setting: Jereboam II (c. 793-753 B.C.) was king of Israel, Uzziah was king of Judah (c. 790-739 B.C.). During a time of wealth & prosperity in Israel. Two years before a great earthquake (c. 762).

Of Interest: The prophets Hosea, Jonah, and Isaiah were Amos' contemporaries.

General Information about the book of AMOS:

Amos was from the southern kingdom of Judah, which made him unwelcome in Israel.
Amos called the people of Israel to repentance.
- Israel had established altars and worshipped idols in Bethel and Dan.
- They were oppressing the poor
- Lack of justice, the judges were accepting bribes

Content Highlights:
- God's Judgment Upon Israel's Enemies (Syria, Philistia, Tyre, Edom, Ammon, and Moab)
- Judgment on Israel and Judah
- Israel's Sin, Guilt, and Punishment
- Five Visions of Judgment
- Restoration of Israel

Seek good, and not evil, that ye may live: and so the LORD, the God of hosts shall be with you, as ye have spoken.

Amos 5:14a

Note:
- Amos is one of the 12 minor prophets (meaning the shorter prophetic books, not that they were less important than major prophets).
- Chronologically, Amos should fall before Hosea.

KEY Verses:
- 2:4-5
- 3:1-2
- 3:7
- 3:1-2
- 4:12-13
- 5:4
- 5:14-15
- 5:24
- 7:7-8
- 8:11
- 8:11-14
- 9:11, 14-15

Theme: Neither Jew or Gentile is immune from God's judgment.

©2023 Wildrose Media

OBADIAH

Literary Style: Prophecy

OLD Testament Book # **31** # of chapters **1**

Author: The prophet Obadiah.

Audience: Nation of Judah, to reassure them that God would judge Edom for their treatment of the Israelites. All future readers of the Bible.

Setting: Obadiah wrote this book following an attack on Jerusalem. It is thought Obadiah was a contemporary of Elijah and Elisha.

Of Interest: Obadiah is the shortest book in the Old Testament.

General Information about the book of OBADIAH:

A prophecy against the nation of Edom.
Edom had not helped Judah when it had been attacked, instead gloated over their defeat.
Edom was located South and East of the Dead Sea.
Obadiah prophecies that Edom will be destroyed and plundered.
The Edomites were descendants of Esau, Jacob's older (twin) brother, who traded his birthright for food.

Content Highlights:

- God Judges Edom
- Edom's Punishment
- The Restoration of Israel

Note:
- *Obadiah* means 'servant of the Lord'.
- There are similarities between Obadiah 1-9 and Jeremiah 49:7-22.

For the day of the Lord is near upon all heathen: as thou hast done, it shall be done unto thee; thy reward shall return upon thine own head.

Obadiah 1:15

KEY Verses:
- Verse 3,4
- Verse 12
- Verse 15
- Verse 17

Theme: God will punish those who harm His people.
What you reap, you will sow.

©2023 Wildrose Media

JONAH

Literary Style: Historical Narrative, Prophecy

OLD Testament Book # **32**   # of chapters **4**

Author → Written in the third person but attributed to Jonah himself. Jonah was from the northern kingdom of Israel, a town called Gath-hepher near Nazareth.

Audience → The Jewish people and all future readers of the Bible.

Setting → During Jereboam II's reign. Jonah is called by God in Israel, flees to the port town of Joppa, boards a ship sailing to Tarshish (Spain), spends time inside a great fish, then finally arrives in Nineveh.

Of Interest → Jonah and Hosea are the only northern kingdom prophets whose writings are in the Bible. Amos was a contemporary of Jonah. Jereboam II ruled Israel from 793 to 753 B.C. (2 Kings 14:25)

General Information about the book of Jonah:

Jonah is different from other prophetic books.
- The book focuses on Jonah's actions, not his prophesies.
- Jonah's prophetic warnings were to a city outside of Israel and Judah.

Nineveh (now called Mosul) was the capital of Assyria (northern Iraq). It was founded by Noah's great grandson, Nimrod.

To Israel's shame the pagan Ninevites repented after hearing Jonah's warning, while the Israelites were repeatedly warned yet continued in their sinful ways.

Content Highlights:
- God Tells Jonah to Warn Nineveh of Coming Destruction
- Jonah Flees from His Calling
- Storm at Sea
- Jonah is Thrown Overboard and is Swallowed by a Great Fish
- Jonah Submits to God and is Vomited onto Dry Land
- Jonah goes to Nineveh
- The Ninevites Repent & Avoid Destruction
- Jonah Questions God's Mercy
- God Rebukes Jonah

Note ←
- During his earthly ministry Jesus mentioned only four prophets by name, Jonah, Daniel, Isaiah, and Zechariah.
- Jonah foreshadowed Jesus' death and resurrection, spending 3 days in the belly of the great fish, as Jesus was 3 days in the heart of the earth.
- *Jonah* means 'dove'.

Salvation is of the Lord.

Jonah 2:9b

KEY Verses ←
- 1:9
- 1:11-17
- 2:1-2
- 2:8-9
- 3:3-5
- 3:10
- 4:1-2
- 4:4

Theme → God's love and mercy extends to Gentiles as well as Jews.

©2023 Wildrose Media

MICAH

Literary Style: Prophecy

OLD Testament Book #: 33
# of chapters: 7

Author: Micah (1:1)

Audience: The Jews in Judah and all future readers of the Bible.

Setting: Micah ministered c. 735-700 B.C. around the same time as Isaiah, Hosea, and Amos. Micah ministered to Judah, Jerusalem, and Samaria for about 55 years.

Of Interest: Micah was from a small town, he had great concern for the poor, weak, and exploited. (2:1-2)

General Information about the book of MICAH:

The people of Judah had been experiencing peace and prosperity but had fallen into moral and spiritual decay. Judges were corrupt, idolatry was everywhere, and the priests valued money over God. They integrated Baal worship and rituals with the God-appointed feasts and sacrifices, corrupting them. Micah is sent to speak words of judgment against this idolatry, corruption, and injustice. He warns of coming judgment against Judah and Samaria. This warning is evidence of God's mercy, He gives them opportunity to repent and be reconciled to Him, rather than destroy them without warning. Micah reminds the people of God's judgment for sin and disobedience, but also gives them hope. God, through Micah renews His promise for a Messiah and for the restoration of Israel.

Micah:
- Proclaims the Assyrian captivity of the Northern Kingdom and the destruction of Jerusalem
- Names Bethlehem as the place of the Messiah's birth
- Message of future deliverance, a reminder of God's promises to Abraham and Israel

Content Highlights:
- God's Judgement on Judah, Samaria and False Prophets
- God's Judgement on the Leaders
- Promise of Deliverance and Restoration

And what doth the Lord require of thee, but to do justly, and to love mercy, and to walk humbly with thy God?

Micah 6:8b

Note:
- The name *Micah* is a shortened form of Micaiah, and means 'who is like God?'
- Micah is one of the 12 books of the Minor Prophets (the book's length, not importance).
- Prophets received messages from God through visions, dreams, oracles.

KEY Verses:
- 1:2, 5
- 2:3
- 2:12-13
- 3:4
- 3:9,12
- 4:1-5
- 5:2
- 5:8-9
- 6:6-8
- 6:13-16
- 7:7-9
- 7:18-20

Theme: God is gracious, merciful, and just; He keeps His promises.

©2023 Wildrose Media

NAHUM

Literary Style: Poetry, Prophecy

OLD Testament Book # **34** # of chapters **3**

Author > Nahum, a prophet and poet.

Audience > Written to the Gentiles living in Nineveh, and all future readers of the Bible. Nahum's only message to Judah was to keep the Lord's Feast Days (1:15).

Setting > Nahum prophesies to Nineveh about 100 years (c. 663-612 B.C.) after Jonah's message. Though they had repented the Ninevites have returned to their wicked ways.

Of Interest > The Northern Kingdom had been conquered by the Assyrians decades earlier (722 B.C.). Judah should have been comforted by the revelation the Assyrians would soon be destroyed.

General Information about the book of NAHUM:

- Nahum is essentially Part 2 of the book of Jonah. God initially withheld His punishment on the Ninevites, but now He executes His righteous judgement and destroys the Assyrian nation.
- Nineveh, the capital city of Assyria is destroyed in 612 B.C. by the Babylonians.
- The book of Nahum is a celebration of divine retribution, payback for the mistreatment of God's people by their enemies.
- Nineveh was considered invincible. It had 100-foot-high walls with a 150-foot-wide moat (60 feet deep) surrounding it. The city was destroyed by water, flooding from the destruction of their protective dams. (see 2:6, 8).
- The remains of Nineveh were not rediscovered until the 19th century.

Content Highlights:

- God's Power and Greatness Extolled
- Nineveh's Destruction Predicted
- The Destruction of Nineveh

The Lord is slow to anger, and great in power; and will not at all acquit the wicked...

Nahum 1:3a

Note >
- Nahum prophesied during the same time period as Habakkuk, Jeremiah, and Zephaniah.
- Nahum's name means *comfort*.
- This book is one of the 12 Minor Prophets.

KEY Verses
- 1:2-3
- 1:6-7
- 1:12-13
- 1:15
- 2:13
- 3:1
- 3:18-19

Theme > God is good and compassionate, but He will not let the guilty go unpunished.

©2023 Wildrose Media

HABAKKUK

Literary Style: Prophecy, Poetry, a Song

OLD Testament Book # **35** # of chapters **3**

Author: The prophet Habakkuk.

Audience: The people of Judah, and all future readers of the Bible.

Setting: Not much is known about Habakkuk, he lived and ministered in Judah.
The events likely occurred at the end of the Assyrian Empire, during the reign of godly King Josiah.

Of Interest: The Babylonians were also known as the Chaldeans.

General Information about the book of HABAKKUK:

Habakkuk was concerned to see the wicked prosper and the righteous suffer.
In this book, Habakkuk asks God about this apparent injustice.
Habakkuk does not address the people of God.
When God reveals His plan to correct Judah and punish Babylon, Habakkuk sings a song of worship.

Content Highlights:

Questions from Habakkuk:
- Why Does God Permit Sin Among His People?
    God Responds
- Why Does God Allow the Unrighteous to Be Successful?
    God Responds
- Habakkuk's Prayer

For the vision is yet for an appointed time, but at the end it shall speak and not lie: though it tarry, wait for it; because it will surely come, it will not tarry.

Habakkuk 2:3

Note:
- Habakkuk was a contemporary of Ezekiel, Daniel, Jeremiah, and Zephaniah.

KEY Verses:
- 1:2
- 1:5-6
- 1:13
- 2:8
- 2:14
- 2:18-20
- 3:2
- 3:17-19

Theme: No one can avoid God's discipline.

©2023 Wildrose Media

ZEPHANIAH

Literary Style: Poetry, Prophecy

OLD Testament Book #: 36
# of chapters: 3

Author: Zephaniah (1:1). He likely prophesied in Judah from 635 – 625 B.C.

Audience: The people of Judah and all future readers of the Bible.

Setting: Zephaniah ministered during the early years of Josiah's reign as king of Judah (640-609 B.C.), before the Law was located and read in 622 B.C. which led to a brief period of revival and reforms.

Of Interest: Zephaniah is a descendant of King Hezekiah. His royal ties likely gave him access to King Josiah.

General Information about the book of ZEPHANIAH:

Zephaniah warns that Judah's final days were near, God's judgment (via Nebuchadnezzar) was at hand.
Zephaniah urged the people of Judah to repent from idolatry and seek God.
Judah had been led by two wicked kings (Ammon and Manasseh), and now sacrificed to Molech, Baal, and other pagan gods.
After their punishment, a remnant would be restored to preserve the line of David, as God promised.

Content Highlights:

- Warning of Destruction
- The Judgment of Judah
- The Judgment of the Gentile Nations
- Jerusalem's Future
- Future Blessings for Jews and Gentiles

Note:
- One of the books of the 12 Minor Prophets.
- Zephaniah was a contemporary of Jeremiah.
- The name Zephaniah means *the Lord has hidden*. As a descendant of Hezekiah, his parents may have had to hide him from evil king Manasseh.

The Lord thy God in the midst of thee is mighty; he will save, he will rejoice over thee with joy...

Zephaniah 3:17a

KEY Verses:
- 1:4-6
- 1:13
- 1:14, 17-18
- 2:3
- 2:6-7
- 2:10-11
- 3:1-2
- 3:12-13
- 3:14-20

Theme: Rebellion against God must be punished. Once cleansed, a remnant of Jews and Gentiles will be fully restored and once again receive God's blessing.

©2023 Wildrose Media

HAGGAI

Literary Style: Poetry, Prophecy

OLD Testament Book #: 37
# of chapters: 2

Author: The prophet Haggai. He may have been over 70 years old when he ministered to Judah, as it seems he saw Solomon's Temple prior to its destruction (2:3).

Audience: The exiled people of Judah and all future readers of the Bible.

Setting: The timing of Haggai's prophesies are not debated as the date for each is provided.

Of Interest: The destruction of the Temple signified God's departure from His people. The reconstruction of God's dwelling place symbolized the Lord's return and presence among His people.

General Information about the book of HAGGAI:

Following Nebuchadnezzar's destruction of the Temple in 586 B.C., Babylon had been conquered by Persia. King Cyrus allowed the Jews to return to Judah and rebuild the Temple. The first (about 50,000) exiles returned in 538 B.C.

Their efforts to rebuild the Temple were slow, hampered by neighboring nations. Haggai and Zephaniah were Sent to Jerusalem to provide spiritual guidance and supervise the Temple reconstruction. Four years after they arrived the Temple was completed.

Haggai had 4 messages for the people.

Content Highlights:
- A Call to Judah to 'Consider Their Ways'
- A Call to Rebuild the Temple
- God Declares His Glory Will Return to the Temple
- Blessings
- God's Message to Zerubbabel

Note:
- Haggai is mentioned in the book of Ezra, along with the prophet Zechariah.
- When given advice from the prophet's Zechariah and Haggai, the governor Zerubbabel obeys. (many kings chose to ignore God's prophets)

Thus saith the Lord of hosts; consider your ways.

Haggai 1:7

KEY Verses:
- 1:7
- 1:9-10
- 1:12
- 2:5
- 2:6-9

Theme: God delights in obedience.

©2023 Wildrose Media

ZECHARIAH

Literary Style: Composite Work, Prophecy

OLD Testament Book # **38** | # of chapters **14**

Author: Zechariah, a prophet and priest born during the Babylonian exile. He was among the first group of Israelites to return from Babylon in 536 B.C. following King Cyrus' decree.

Audience: The Jews in Jerusalem, Judah, and all future readers of the Bible.

Setting: Events take place after the Babylonian exiles had returned to Israel in 538 B.C. The visions began c. November 520 B.C, chapters 9-14 take place after the Temple had been rebuilt.

Of Interest: Zechariah is the most frequently quoted prophetic book in the New Testament. It contains several prophecies about the coming Messiah.

General Information about the book of ZECHARIAHI:

Zechariah encourages the people to continue rebuilding the Temple in Jerusalem. The foundations were laid, but nothing else had been constructed. By 516 B.C. the Temple had been completed (Ezra 6:15).

He gives words of encouragement- Israel's enemies will be overcome, Israel will be restored to the Lord, and all nations will worship the Lord.

This book contains prophecies about the Messiah and eschatology (end times) but also repentance, salvation, and holy living.

Content Highlights:

Preface

The book is broken into 3 sections.

1. The Eight Visions (chapters 1-6). An angel leads Zechariah through the visions, and interprets them. The visions use symbolism, allegories, and signs to present their message. Some of these signs are also used in the books of Revelation and Isaiah.
2. The Four Messages (chapters 7 & 8). These messages are given after the Temple had been rebuilt.
3. Two Oracles (chapters 9-14). Prophesies concerning the Messiah, his rejection, the restoration of God's people, and the coming Kingdom of God.

"Turn ye unto me, saith the Lord of hosts, and I will turn unto you saith the Lord of hosts".

Zechariah 1:3b

Note:
- The book of Zechariah is classified as one of the Minor Prophets (in terms of size, not importance).
- Zechariah was a contemporary of Haggai.
- The name *Zechariah* means 'Yahweh remembers."
- More than 29 men in the OT are named Zechariah.

KEY Verses:
- 1:3, 17
- 2:10-11
- 5:5-11
- 7:8-14
- 8:6-8
- 9:9
- 10:6
- 11:7-17
- 13:7-9

Theme: God is faithful to His covenant promises.

©2023 Wildrose Media

MALACHI

Literary Style: Q & A, Prophetic Oracles

OLD Testament Book # 39 | # of chapters 4

Author: Most scholars agree the prophet Malachi wrote this book, though some give Ezra or Mordecai credit.

Audience: Written to the Jews who had returned to Israel after the Babylonian captivity.

Setting: No date is included, approximately 100 years since the exiles had returned to Judah from Babylon. The Temple had been rebuilt and rituals held, but the priests and people were violating God's laws.

Of Interest: Clues to the date Malachi was written are found by comparing it with Nehemiah and Ezra. Other clues are the Temple (rebuilt 515 BC) and Persian words (Persia ruled Judea 538-333 BC).

General Information about the book of MALACHI:

Malachi is the last of the minor prophets.

Like Haggai and Zechariah, Malachi is written after the Jewish exile. These three books warn about repeating the sins of their fathers. The other minor prophets warn about the coming destruction of Judah, Israel, or other nations.

The people lived as though outward rituals were enough to comply with God's will, but Malachi points out that their hypocrisy, arrogance, and false worship are sinful violations of God's covenant.

Only a remnant of these Israelites feared the Lord and had hope for a coming Messiah.

Malachi is the final book of the Old Testament Period, 400 years of silence before John the Baptist appears.

The final prophecy recorded in the Old Testament is Malachi 1:1-46 (written c. 424 B.C.).

Content Highlights:

Chapter 1 God's Love for His People
Chapter 1-2 The Disrespect and Improper Worship of the Priests
Chapter 2-3 The Unfaithfulness of the People
Chapter 3-4 Hope for Israel's Future
Chapter 4 The Day of the Lord

Behold, I will send my messenger, and he shall prepare the way before me: and the LORD, whom ye seek, shall suddenly come to his temple, even the messenger of the covenant, whom ye delight in: behold, he shall come, saith the LORD of hosts.

Malachi 3:1

- Malachi means "my messenger".
- The meaning of chapter 4:5 which states Elijah will come before the day of the Lord is debated. Some believe this was fulfilled by John the Baptist (though he was not Elijah reincarnated John 1:21), others believe Elijah will reappear, perhaps as one of the two witnesses mentioned in Rev. 11:1-19.

Note

KEY Verses

- 1:2-5
- 1:11, 14
- 2:7-9
- 3:2-5
- 3:6, 7
- 3:16-18
- 4:1, 5-6

Theme: God loves His people and will deliver them as He promised.

©2023 Wildrose Media

Wildrose Media website
- Home - Page

Faith Family Fun Blog
Homeschool Tips +

Wildrose Media website
- Shop - Page

Additional books from Wildrose Media, available on Amazon:

Sermon Notebook
Kids Ages 9-12 years
Wooden Cross cover

Sermon Notebook
Kids Ages 6-8 years
Bunny pattern cover

The Birth of Jesus
Coloring Book

The Story of Easter
Coloring Book
Blue cover

Bible Teaching Sheets
OLD TESTAMENT - KJV

Bible Teaching Sheets
NEW TESTAMENT - KJV

Friendship and Freedom
Story of the Statue of Liberty

100 Questions to Ask Myself
Vol.1 - pink cover

Ultimate Fishing Journal
for Kids Vol. 1

Ultimate Fishing Journal
for Girls - pink cover

Headache Diary, 5"x 6"
Symptom Notebook

Dutch Boy & Girl
Small Notebook 5"x6"

The above book QR codes are Amazon Affiliate links,
I may receive compensation from purchases made using these links,
at no additional cost to you.

Made in United States
Orlando, FL
22 September 2025